EDGE
BOOKS

MINI-BEAST WARS

ASSASSIN BUG VS OGRE-FACED SPIDER

BY ALICIA Z. KLEPEIS

WHEN CUNNING HUNTERS COLLIDE

raintree

a Capstone company — publishers for children

Raintree is an imprint of Capstone Global Library Limited, a company incorporated in England and Wales having its registered office at 264 Banbury Road, Oxford, OX2 7DY – Registered company number: 6695582

www.raintree.co.uk
myorders@raintree.co.uk

ISBN 978 1 4747 1085 5
20 19 18 17 16 15
10 9 8 7 6 5 4 3 2 1

British Library Cataloguing in Publication Data
A full catalogue record for this book is available from the British Library.

Editorial Credits
Aaron Sautter, editor; Russell Griesmer, designer; Jo Miller, media researcher;
Katy LaVigne, production specialist

The publisher would like to thank Christiane Weirauch, Professor of Entomology at University of California, Riverside for her help creating this book.

Photo Credits
Alamy: Daniel Borzynski, 15, Steve Bloom Images, 27, (top); Minden Pictures: Kazuo Unno, Nature Production, 23; Newscom: Arco Images G/picture alliance/Huetter, C., 25, Minden Pictures/Ch"len Lee, 24, Minden Pictures/Stephen Dalton, 19, Photoshot/NHPA/Gerhard Koertner, 29, Photoshot/NHPA/Nick Garbutt, 17; Science Source: ANT Photo Library, 21, John Serrao, 11, Shutterstock: Melinda Fawver, Cover (left), 5, 7, 9, 22, Paul Looyen, Cover (right), 7, Peter Waters, 4, Robyn Butler, 6, Tom Grundy, 27, (bottom); SuperStock: NaturePL, 13

Design Elements
Capstone and Shutterstock

CONTENTS

WELCOME TO MINI-BEAST WARS!

Some mini-beasts are ferocious hunters.
They search for **prey**, kill it and eat it. These fierce
predators often have clear advantages over others.
But in Mini-Beast Wars, that's not the case. These
flesh-eating killers are all equipped with fangs, **venom**,
sticky webs and other deadly weapons. In Mini-Beast Wars
you never know which hunter will end up victorious!

prey animal hunted by another animal for food
predator animal that hunts other animals for food
venom poisonous liquid produced by some animals

DEADLY HUNTERS

You're about to watch an Assassin Bug and an Ogre-Faced Spider in a fight to the death. But first you'll learn how these killer mini-beasts match up against each other. You'll discover their deadly weapons and how they fight in combat. Finally, you'll watch from a front row seat as they fight it out!

THE COMBATANTS

Assassin bugs and ogre-faced spiders may not encounter each other often in the wild. But they do share some territory. Both live in warm climates in North and South America, Africa, Asia and Australia.

Although these predators thrive in warm temperatures, they are found in a variety of **habitats**. Assassin bugs live in grasslands, forests, and even deserts. Meanwhile, ogre-faced spiders are often found in **bushlands** and tropical forests.

Both of these hunters can destroy other insects easily. An assassin bug's bite can **paralyse** a cockroach in just 4 seconds! And the ogre-faced spider eats all sorts of insects from beetles to butterflies.

Assassin bugs and ogre-faced spiders don't always battle each other. They usually munch on smaller insects. But you never know – when they're hungry, they'll take food wherever they can find it!

THERE ARE NEARLY 7,000 SPECIES
OF ASSASSIN BUGS IN THE WORLD.

habitat natural place and conditions in which a plant
or animal lives
bushland dry area of land where trees and shrubs grow
paralyse cause a loss of the ability to control
the muscles

SIZE AND SPEED

The wheel bug is one of the world's largest assassin bugs. It can measure up to 3.8 centimetres (1.5 inches) long, or about the size of a large paperclip. Assassin bugs move slowly. They walk with a bouncy step at about 1 to 3 cm (0.4 to 1.2 in) per second. They are also slow and clumsy fliers. But the slow walking speed of these mini-beasts can be deceiving. These hunters can move especially fast when striking at prey. An assassin bug's strike happens in less than 0.1 second. That's faster than people can blink their eyes!

The ogre-faced spider is larger than an assassin bug. Including its legs, this scary spider can be up to 7.6 cm (3 in) long. The ogre-faced spider is also much faster than an assassin bug. With its long legs, the spider can run up to 10 cm (4 in) per second.

The spider's speed is seen when catching its prey. This hunter can strike in just one thousandth of a second. That's 10 times faster than a lightning bolt! The spider's speed is a huge advantage when catching prey – and during a fight.

RATING 2

ASSASSIN BUG:
slow mover,
fast striker

RATING 4

OGRE-FACED
SPIDER:
fast mover,
super-fast striker

FIERCE FACT

THE SCIENTIFIC NAME FOR OGRE-FACED SPIDERS IS
DEINOPIS, WHICH MEANS "TERRIBLE APPEARANCE".
SOME PEOPLE THINK THESE SPIDERS' HUGE EYES
MAKE THEM LOOK LIKE OGRES.

ASSASSIN BUG DEFENCES

Like most insects, the assassin bug has an **exoskeleton**. This hard armour-like covering helps protect it during an attack. The wheel bug's jagged body armour is especially sturdy. The teeth-like projections on the mini-beast's back may make it difficult for a predator to eat it.

As well as being hard and tough, an assassin bug's exoskeleton serves another purpose. Its colour enables the mini-beast to either warn or hide from enemies. Some assassin bugs have bright colours to warn predators that they're dangerous. Other assassin bugs have grey, black or brown bodies. These colours provide excellent **camouflage**. These mini-beasts often blend in easily with plants. This helps them to stay hidden from both predators and prey.

exoskeleton structure on the outside of an animal that gives it support
camouflage colouring or covering that makes animals, people and objects look like their surroundings

ASSASSIN BUG:
tough exoskeleton,
great camouflage

FIERCE FACT

IF DISTURBED, SOME ASSASSIN BUGS
CAN SPRAY A STINGING MIST THAT
CHASES AWAY PREDATORS.

OGRE-FACED SPIDER DEFENCES

The ogre-faced spider has camouflage of its own. Its brown colouring and long slender legs make it look like a stick. This makes the spider hard for other mini-beasts to spot. This is especially true when it lies stretched out on a branch.

The ogre-faced spider's best defence is its excellent vision. Its two huge eyes give it better night vision than cats or even owls! Its great vision gives the spider a huge advantage over its enemies.

Ogre-faced spiders have one other incredible defence. If a leg becomes caught or damaged, these spiders can shed the injured limb and keep moving. Special body parts inside the spider then work to reduce any bleeding. This process is called **autotomy**, and it can be very useful in a fight.

autotomy ability of some animals to safely shed a damaged or trapped body part

RATING

3

OGRE-FACED SPIDER:
excellent vision,
good camouflage

ASSASSIN BUG WEAPONS

The assassin bug is a killing machine. It has many dangerous weapons to use when hunting and fighting. Many of these mini-beasts can extend their front legs outwards to grasp prey. Some assassin bugs have spines on these legs that help them hold onto victims.

The assassin bug's mouthparts are similar to a mosquito's. They are specialized for stabbing and sucking. Some insects use their **mandibles** for chomping. But the assassin bug's mandibles form part of its straw-like **rostrum**. The rostrum is strong and beak-like. It can stab right through its prey's exoskeleton.

The assassin bug's rostrum is dangerous. But its deadliest weapon is its venom. The venom can paralyse prey within seconds and liquefy its insides.

mandibles strong mouthparts used for chewing
rostrum strong, piercing mouthpart used by some insects for hunting prey

ASSASSIN BUG:
sharp rostrum,
deadly venom

FIERCE FACT

WHEN NOT IN USE, THE ASSASSIN BUG CAN
TUCK ITS ROSTRUM NEATLY INTO A NARROW
GROOVE BETWEEN ITS FRONT LEGS.

OGRE-FACED SPIDER WEAPONS

The ogre-faced spider is a very scary-looking predator. Its two long fangs can easily pierce an enemy's flesh. The fangs are also important tools for injecting the spider's venom into its prey. The venom paralyses prey very quickly. Victims are usually unable to move when the spider begins munching on them!

The spider's venom is nasty stuff. But this crafty hunter uses another impressive weapon. It makes a postage-stamp sized web that spreads out like a net. The web is made of special **cribellum silk**. This sticky silk snags and sticks to insects' legs. The spider uses its special net to trap its prey with lightning speed.

cribellum silk type of spider silk made of tiny fibres that has a woolly appearance; insects easily get tangled and caught in this type of silk

OGRE-FACED SPIDER:
wicked web

FIERCE FACT

IF THE OGRE-FACED SPIDER DOESN'T USE ITS WEB DURING THE NIGHT, IT WILL EAT IT. THE SPIDER THEN MAKES A NEW NET THE FOLLOWING NIGHT.

ASSASSIN BUG ATTACK STYLE

The assassin bug is a careful hunter. It uses its antennae to sense vibrations. Once prey is found, this mini-beast carefully creeps up on it. The hunter moves in a bouncy and irregular way. When the assassin bug is close enough to its prey, it strikes viciously. The predator plunges its sharp rostrum repeatedly into its prey's body.

But stabbing its prey is only part of the assassin bug's attack. It also squirts venom into its victim's body. The assassin bug's powerful venom starts to act in just 3 to 5 seconds. Within 15 seconds the prey can't move and its insides quickly turn to liquid. The assassin bug then sucks out the soupy guts before moving on to find its next victim.

ASSASSIN BUG:
sharp rostrum,
deadly venom

**FIERCE
FACT**

THE ASSASSIN BUG'S SALIVA WORKS AS AN ANAESTHETIC.
IN MOST CASES ITS PREY DOESN'T FEEL PAIN.

anaesthetic substance that reduces sensitivity to pain

OGRE-FACED SPIDER ATTACK STYLE

The ogre-faced spider is a patient hunter. Its camouflaged body helps keep it hidden from prey. The spider holds its woven net in its four front legs. Its head dangles down as it waits for prey to pass by. The spider's body has tiny hairs that can sense when insects are moving near by.

The ogre-faced spider stays perfectly still as it waits. When prey touches one of the net's anchoring threads, the spider knows its next meal is within reach. Faster than lightning, the ogre-faced spider casts its net over its victim. The net quickly contracts and tangles the unlucky insect in its sticky threads. The spider then injects venom into its victim with its sharp fangs. Lightning-quick reflexes and web wrapping skills make the ogre-faced spider a fearsome predator.

OGRE-FACED SPIDER:
rapid prey-wrapper

FIERCE FACT

SOME OGRE-FACED SPIDERS HAVE ANOTHER
METHOD TO FIND PREY. THEY SPREAD
DROPPINGS ON THE GROUND UNDER THEIR WEB,
WHICH DRIES WHITE. IF AN INSECT THEN RUNS
ACROSS THE DROPPINGS AT NIGHT, THE SPIDER
CAN SEE ITS PREY AS THOUGH A TORCH IS
SHINING ON IT.

GET READY TO RUMBLE!

Are you prepared for a ferocious fight? These two
hungry flesh-eating mini-beasts are looking for their
next meal. But they're about to collide in a fierce
battle. In one corner is the gut-piercing assassin bug!
It's sneaky and packs a secret hidden weapon. In the
other corner is its fearsome foe – the ogre-faced spider!
Even its name sounds frightening. It's a lightning-quick
killer. Nobody knows which of these foes will win. But
one thing is certain – these fearsome hunters will keep
battling until the bitter end.

You've got a front row seat. So grab your favourite
snack, turn the page and get ready to enjoy the battle!

ONE LAST THING...

This fight is made up, just like in your favourite films. These two mini-beasts may occasionally fight each other in nature, but it's hard to say who would really win. However, we know they're ferocious fighters. So if you like a good battle, this should be a great show!

GUTS AND GLORY

It's night-time in the forest. An ogre-faced spider has found a perfect spot to hide. His stick-like body blends in perfectly with the nearby branches. He's nearly invisible to other creatures. He hangs upside down and scans the area with his huge, bulging eyes. Between his front legs he holds his trap, a bluish-white web of special silk.

Near by an assassin bug is also on the prowl. He's hungry and hopes to find a tasty meal. His antennae twitch, sensing the movement of other insects creeping below him. Soon he sees a spider's web gleaming in the faint moonlight. He unpacks his deadly rostrum from its tucked-away position. He's ready for action.

The ogre-faced spider's bulging eyeballs peer into the darkness. Finally, it spots the smaller assassin bug. The spider tracks his prey, patiently but with purpose. He is waiting for it to come closer – so that he can strike!

But the assassin bug has its own plans. He hopes to turn the spider into a midnight meal. The assassin bug tries plucking on the spider's web. Bad choice! He touched one of the web's "trip wires". The spider quickly swoops down to attack the assassin bug.

FIERCE FACT

THREAD-LEGGED MINI-BEASTS SOMETIMES LURE SPIDERS BY PLUCKING THE THREADS OF THEIR WEBS. THIS DRAWS THE SPIDERS CLOSER, ALLOWING THE THREAD-LEGGED MINI-BEASTS TO STRIKE.

But the assassin bug fights back. The two hunters tussle. Each lashes out at the other with all its might. The assassin bug tries to jab the ogre-faced spider with his beak-like rostrum, but misses. During the deadly duel, one of the spider's legs is torn off! The ogre-faced spider staggers back, reeling from his nasty injury. The bleeding quickly stops, thanks to the spider's internal shut-off valve. He'll grow a new leg later. Right now, it's time to get back to the fight.

For a moment it looks like the assassin bug has the advantage. But then he makes a fatal mistake. He wanders underneath his spider foe. In a flash, the ogre-faced spider casts his special web over his prey. The assassin bug is trapped. He tries once more to stab the spider with his rostrum. But the ogre-faced spider acts fast to avoid being speared by his foe. Keeping the assassin bug as far away as possible, the cunning spider quickly wraps his prey in layers of sticky silk.

FIERCE FACT

SOME TYPES OF SPIDER SILK
ARE STRONGER THAN STEEL.

A FEW TYPES OF ASSASSIN BUGS ARE CALLED "KISSING BUGS". THESE BUGS FEED ON THE BLOOD OF ANIMALS AND PEOPLE. THEY ARE CALLED KISSING BUGS BECAUSE THEY TEND TO DRAW BLOOD FROM THE FACES OF THEIR VICTIMS.

Before long the assassin bug is bound tightly like a mummy. He can do nothing. Knowing his prey can't move, the ogre-faced spider injects his victim with paralysing venom. The assassin bug is powerless. He can't use his legs or rostrum anymore. He has lost the battle. Death comes swiftly for the assassin bug. Soon the ogre-faced spider will be slurping up the dissolved innards of his prey. He'll be eating well tonight!

GLOSSARY

anaesthetic substance that reduces sensitivity to pain

autotomy ability of some animals to safely shed a damaged or trapped body part

bushland dry area of land where trees and shrubs grow

camouflage colouring or covering that makes animals, people and objects look like their surroundings

cribellum silk type of spider silk made of tiny fibres that has a woolly appearance; insects easily get tangled and caught in this type of silk

exoskeleton structure on the outside of an animal that gives it support

habitat natural place and conditions in which a plant or animal lives

mandibles strong mouthparts used for chewing

paralyse cause a loss of the ability to control the muscles

predator animal that hunts other animals for food

prey animal hunted by another animal for food

rostrum strong, piercing mouthpart used by some insects for hunting prey

venom poisonous liquid produced by some animals

READ MORE

Amazing Animal Predators (Animal Superpowers),
John Townsend (Raintree, 2013)

Super Spiders (Walk on the Wild Side), Charlotte Guillain
(Raintree, 2014)

Tarantula vs Bird (Predator vs Prey),
Mary Meinking Chambers (Raintree, 2012)

WEBSITES

www.britannica.com/animal/assassin-bug
Find out more about the many species of assassin bugs, their
features and their behaviours.

www.sciencechannel.com/tv-shows/monster-bug-wars/
videos/monster-bug-wars-ogre-vs-assassin/
Watch as an assassin bug tries to take on an ogre-faced
spider and see which one wins in the end.

INDEX